If All This Never Happened

If All This Never Happened

Vicky Morris

SOUTHWORD*editions*

First published in 2021
by Southword Editions
The Munster Literature Centre
Frank O'Connor House, 84 Douglas Street
Cork, Ireland

Set in Adobe Caslon 11pt

ISBN 978-1-905002-85-6

Contents

For Lesley, Matilda & Little Jo

Lesley

i.m Lesley Ann Downey 1954 - 1964

Sometimes I tell the story of my namesake,
of how my mother (when she was Nurse Margaret)
met a young policeman in the hospital staff room
raw from listening to the evidence at Chester Assizes;

the 16-minute tape they'd had to sit through, found
in an old suitcase, station lost property, its ticket
in the spine of a prayer book. How he sat and wept
in his dark uniform, and she made him sugary tea.

How I was named for Lesley, for her ten short years,
for her joy at the Ancoats Boxing Day Fair, for her
wide-eyed trust of the world, her tartan frock, pink cardie
and red shoes, for how she called to God for Mummy.

And I picture my mother sat there listening,
her hand on his hand, the other on her belly, me not yet
kicking. She said she wanted to bring her back,
she wanted to bring her home.

Where We Used to Live

2 Winston Close,
the end of a council row, me dangling
on tiptoes over the high garden wall –
I could lean over it now. Once the littlest
left alone eating soil out back, Lorna
tightrope-walking the fence, the ambulance
the time she slipped either side of the slats,
the bloody seashell; her finger trapped
in the hinges of the kitchen door.

Just down from the stilted house
where a woman strangled her daughter
with a pair of tights, and the posh guy
Dad sold his car to, who did his girlfriend
in with a brick. Mum in the dark
for hours, with just one candle
and no coins for the meter, while we slept
across the tiny landing in the coldest room
with its lonely view out to sea.

If you see people outside
looking in, maybe taking pictures on their phones,
they might be talking like this – about the lives
they once lived in your home. All the things
that didn't make sense or go to plan. One day,
you too might pull up in a car outside, remember
who ate the soil, who sat by candlelight,
who chased who around the garden
with a mop or a carving knife.

Mechanisms

My brother clicked his hair in front of the TV,
curled a clump around fingers, leaving one strand free
to hook under his nail and pull across the coil like a bow
that snapped back, his keratin knuckle crack.

I sucked my thumb, walked around the house,
as if inside the thrum of my mother's belly, appeased
by the suction and scratching of cloth. At first a ribbon
like a violin calm against my nose. Then, over time

a blue polka-dot dress, scraps of other clothes. Until
adolescence loomed, and I let go. But even now, my fingertips
seek out the right direction in the fine rows of a soft polyester.
The stim; that tiny ecstasy of relief in its rubbing together,

that takes me back to a house of unseen fires
where I smooth my cindered mind to sleep, and my sister
snuffs the flames with her teeth across the knuckle
of her index finger, where you can still see the mark.

The Scab

I don't have to put my hand up in class anymore,
pretending to have been abroad, or to know the answer
to any question that says I'm waving, not drowning.

I don't have to sit spotlit when asked to read aloud in English,
with no peristalsis from brain to lips. Or shrink like Alice
from each attempt, my stupid jammed naked into each syllable.

There's no need to make up stories for parents' evening,
or about why I'm not going on the trip to London, or
the reason I haven't taken my pumps off after PE.

I no longer walk past my house on the way home from school,
around to the back ginnel, or open kitchen cupboards wondering
what to make from flour and custard powder, or Marmite.

I don't count coins for the Chinese chippy, or steal 50p
from the sponsor money. Nor do I babysit for the kids
who live on Kraft Single and strawberry jam sandwiches.

No badly cut fringe that hides the scab I can't stop picking.
No Sunday baths, second in the water, Mum wringing out hair
like a cloth. No last thing at night scrubbing grubby collars

on school shirts, or being chased by knuckles and a mop.
And I will never stand on the front path again, most nights,
looking to see my father swaying slowly up the street.

What I Remember about Your Forgetting

"The fact that one can lose the greater part of a lifetime has peculiar, uncanny horror."
Oliver Sacks, on Korsakoff's Syndrome

10

I'm ten, we are standing on either side of the hospital bed.
He's serious when he looks between the two of us and says
Now, which is Vicky, and which is Lorna?
Mum hasn't warned us, she doesn't understand it herself.

So we think it's funny, even more so when he gets up,
takes his suit jacket from the locker and announces –
I'm off down the pub. We watch his skinny, pyjamaed legs
disappear down the corridor, shoulder pads two sizes too big.

11

We are finding things to amuse us about our dad's abduction
into the Twilight Zone. While his replacement in thinner form
takes a break from dissecting the tiny portions on his plate,
wanders off again to count the coins in his jacket pocket,

we move things about nearby, a little each time.
We want to see if he notices where his knife is, why
the salt cellar is standing on top of the butter dish.
We wait, but he never does.

14

Dad is a relic, all bone and blank slate, his words read
from an autocue no one else can see. He asks the date a lot,
the year lost on him every time. He tells the joke he always does
when he sees me dressed up. I answer with the punchline.

15

On rare nights in, he sits with a can labelling things, songs
taped from the radio, books he's re-covered. I watch from the door,
wondering, should I ask him – *where are you?* I never do.

16

I've left home. Now Dad is an answering machine message
that replays sometimes when the phone rings. He posts out a script
he's perfecting through letters, his pen on a loop.

20

Mum, from a hospital phone, says *Your dad's off.*
She hates fuss. I wait for Lorna to come and drive us back in time
to sit beside our father's bed again.

I think of that final call – *were you there?*
Were you there at all? I only remember coughing,
something about last orders being called.

Sending You to Meet Mum

I've told her to stay put, to just wait
until you see her and say *Margaret* –

You'll know her by her beige anorak,
by her rounded shoulders, hunched
from years of stooping low
over sinks of holy water,
bleaching the everyday
out of kitchen cloths,
made from old vests and knickers,
over bath tubs, swirling together
the heavy fabric of three children
and an absent father.

You'll know Margaret
by her restless, disjointed shuffle,
forever trying to balance
in her own gravity.
And when you greet her
don't mind if her smile is shy,
her teeth hidden – she doesn't like to show
the gap her father left at just thirteen.
Don't try to shake hands,
she'll not want to.

She'll probably give you
a clumsy hug,
turning her face away
or clutch your arm,
with hands so callused,
as a child, I'd try to catch her still
for long enough
to touch the cracks
and marvel
at the toughness of human skin.

Pause

If you were to film him in full swing
at a family gathering, out with colleagues,

at dinner with friends, everyone listening
to how considered, how modest, how easily

he holds the room, if you were to capture it all,
like the good wife, and then, sift through the frames

ready to pause, you might catch, in among
the gestures, the punchlines, the nods and applause –

the delight of the dupe, the now-you-see-him cameo,
the upturned corners of someone else's mouth.

Sea Road

(Summer of '85)

Remember the night you and Lorn walked back this way,
past the jangling cluster of amusement arcades, the bingo caller's
muffled boom on the mic, the slot-machine beeps and flashing lights,

then the long quiet stretch of Sea Road. Remember the man
who stopped his car, not once but twice, pretended to fiddle
behind a torch-lit bonnet, and you saw his open fly,

his hand offering up his cock like a fairground prize
to two young girls in beach dresses. Lorn still chattering,
heedless of the whisper in your ten-year-old throat,

and you daren't look back or turn off the road.
Then up ahead, you see a shape in the dark, that same car
waiting, bonnet raised, headlights off, engine ticking,

the dim glow of torchlight. But this time, he's upped
his game. And now you are running, Lorn pulling you
down this long, empty road, running like the dark

is closing in behind you, like it's stroking the backs
of your legs, running from the edge of something sharp
and faceless, until you burst into the hall, gasping, out of breath.

Mum shouting – *What, what is it!?*
Both of you mute, moving along a road somewhere.
The dark of a car boot, your mouths gagged shut.

Visit to a Friend

(Winter 1991)

There she is, that younger you –
not long seventeen. Leaning against the news stand
in the winter sun, while you drive past
South Kensington tube twenty-two years on.
She's waiting for the uncle of her friend Megan,

whose parents, the spring before, let her rent
the box room overlooking their chessboard lawn.
The acupuncturist uncle who'd visit from the Big Smoke,
who spoke with a soft voice. Talked of yin and yang,
of Qi, the rhythms of the body. The uncle who understood

she didn't come from a place where a mother sets the table
for breakfast, and family portraits sit smug on the walls.
The uncle who, when she moved out, invited her
to come for treatment in London Town, hippy-shop
in Camden, try sushi on Portobello Road.

And now, she's standing watching the traffic
where her future-self is driving past. In a few hours,
she'll be tipsy at a party in his apartment block,
sipping Prosecco like lemonade, laughing like she knows
what's what. After, she'll learn what a futon is,

push the *f* from her lips in giggles, because she thinks
it's a funny word for a bed. And when he asks
if she's okay sharing it, she'll comment
on how wide it is. Then drift off, fully dressed
on that icy night, not long before he'll wake her up

with the draught from lifted covers, and he'll press
his cold hardness into the small of her back.
She'll freeze at the edge of the sea of mattress,
then push him away, and say – *I'm sleeping*
and, thankfully, that will be enough.

But the next day, she'll wake to a different kind of chill.
And as it all replays again like a film, you'll realise
she's still standing there, shivering in his treatment room,
while he scolds her like a child, for not wanting
to undress for his needles.

Soulmates (Inbox)

Yes, I did leave you waiting for me,
sat and watched and took you in,
compared you to the pictures you posted, imagined
your mouth form the shape of the words you typed;
your lips a little wet, your jaw soft and loose. Yes,
I did trace the contours of your caramel skin,
let my eyes unzip the length of your boots.

And while I studied your small frame, and you
shuffled those curves from foot to foot, wondering
whether to give up, I did pretend to play
with my phone, and it took a photo of you
from the café opposite the stop where you stood.
And yes, I know sending it to you, as you got on the bus,
was, perhaps, a step too far.

Joy

(22nd May 2017)

When the photos of the dead came in, we looked
at their smiling faces on the TV, how they had brimmed
with possibility, hands clasped in school uniforms.

This was meant for girls. A grenade thrown into the heart
of joy. A reminder that freedom is risky. Once offered,
the world is waiting in ways we cannot anticipate.

But joy is raring to go, so a parent makes a thousand
tiny compromises, watches her inch forwards, a climber
in a harness, impossible to keep in check.

In her first uncertain ascents from the nest, she is
wrapped in incantations of *Be careful,*
Stay with friends, Text for a lift.

Sometimes, a mother, father, has to trust the world
will be kind to their girl in her party clothes, testing
how it feels to be grown.

In the streets of Raqqa joy walks discretely in black,
forbidden to gather while her children play in parks.
To wear scent, talk loudly, is punished.

She will not throw back her head and laugh
into sunlight. Her windows are kept shrouded
so she cannot be glimpsed, even in houses.

And yet, she is still here, behind closed doors,
telling us – *I stand in front of the mirror and smile,*
so I don't forget how.

Ward 2

(Weston Park Hospital)

We are taking up beds,
bodies with the same lead weights
on shoulders we have become unsure of.
The four of us, ladies in Ward 2 waiting,
with our drips and PICCs, and cannulated veins,
wondering when we can go home again.

Maureen forgets to take her tablets.
The nurses scold with laughter.
She offers back giggles from 70 years earlier.
Ashrita cries over a text from her ex.
She had a tooth pulled yesterday.
They give her morphine for the pain.

Denise is the most cheerful.
She is waiting for the okay on a final trial,
asks us all to order bacon for her
when breakfast comes around.
You wouldn't get this at the Northern General
she jokes, chomping it down.

Her husband, Brian, is the Daily Mail newshound.
He soapboxes the corner well past visiting hours,
says he's voting UKIP on Thursday,
says the money should be spent
on cancer drugs, on anything
that could save his wife.

Us

We hold everything in,
everything up. That is, unless

we're showing everything off.
Then we're plunged to half-cupped,

nothing but bravado, barely
the areola covered up. Some

can't run without us, we start them
young in training sizes. But

when we're not strapped on,
we're just two fabric cups, no use

for carrying much, costing a lot.
But not for those who laugh

at the idea of us, or look on us
with mistrust. And there are those

for whom, once we meant
something else, now we hide

a little
of what they've lost.

Treatment

At times, he'll bring out the comedy from it all,
like how he waited hospital hours and succumbed to the soup
that was more like the sauce that comes with baked beans.

He'll tell you things like this, while you wince
as his fingertips become nerve-heavy thumb prints,
rubbing moisture into the red-raw winter of your skin.

Once a week, you'll take a seat while he stands
to pick through matted curls with a hair grip, to see what
he can salvage, his shoulders sore from stooping.

And every third week, he'll rub your feet to distract you
from the pain of the ice cap's -22, and they'll pump you
as you watch, with pesticides, clear and red.

On Tuesdays, tired, he'll wear gloves that never fit,
to clean the line that connects arm to heart, and secure the bung
like a rolled-up cigarette, while all the time you bark instructions.

Like in those first weeks, months before, when he'll lift you
in and out of bed (the way the nurse says is best) and he won't sit
in peace and rest, until you are sleeping.

He'll be your left arm, and the movement of the broom you'll use
to knit back nerves, circling shoulder to elbow in a curve on the floor,
his eyes willing you a little more every time.

He'll remove your paper knickers, your chest padded
and bandaged, and you'll shower for the first time, balanced,
between IV stand and him.

And days before, when the surgeon walks in, he'll come alive
working through the questions you typed, making notes
as he goes, because he knows you'll forget everything else said

after they tell you, one week before you go under, that the MRI
measured 5, not the ultrasound 2.4, and they will have to
take it all. The lymph nodes in your arm. The chance of more.

That's when he will be holding you,
like when he'll tell you
he will still think you're beautiful.

And you will feel it.
You will feel it.

Lounge

The nurse says they should've given me a line-in
the first time, straight to my heart.
Now the veins in my arm grow hard.

FEC chemo is the worst, she says.
We'll sort it for next time. *Then you won't have me*
here again. She smiles, meaning

there'll be no more need to check
if FEC is leaking into tissue. I busy myself,
in the bubble of my pastel recliner,

move through settings for legs and back,
look out across the bow of this sterile ship,
thankful it looks so effortless, on course.

Most scroll phones, heated pillows
propping up wrists, loved ones sat crooked
on hard chairs. All of us watched over

by the daytime TV personalities smiling
their synchronised blessings from three screens,
and the tea trolley keeps on doing the rounds.

This could be some starship old people's home,
where we've paid good money to be drip-fed youth,
but most of us are too young to look the part.

I forget where we are when a little boy
from another ward whizzes in
with a bald head and aeroplane arms.

Garden

(Chemo Summer, 2015)

With pesticide lungs I breathe her in,
a heady sea of sweet peas, tea rose, geranium, jasmine.
Our fast dividing soils have found a way
to germinate;
she comes into being –
perennial, I pass away.

Two years ago I planted the wisp of a clematis,
dreamed she'd creep up the fir tree. This year,
she weaves a ladder of purple stars,
and the honeysuckles have finally kissed the air
with their sticky lips, and the raspberries blush,
the herbs zing, stems grow wings and bulbs push up
from everywhere. Only the rhubarb sulks
under leaves that shield my sun-shy baby skin.

Now I must operate with gloves,
work her cells without getting cuts.
Her plagues are greenfly, slugs,
a neighbour's black and white cat,
the bindweed that suffocates all it clasps,
with its delicate white petals that ask to be kept,
but I rip at the roots because its nature, if left,
will grow and grow and grow.

Sometimes I think of this –
wonder what might be hibernating,
waiting for a spring where it might seed again.
Then I'm absorbed in all the green again,
making a bird's nest
from my falling hair.

German Train

I wish my mind was like this German train,
with its neat fold-up storage, deep luggage racks,
easy-reach wall hooks. Plenty of leg room.
Each seat with its own plug socket,
little boxes attached for all the rubbish.

And wide aisleways, no waiting to pass
the food trolley. A separate dining carriage
for pancakes and coffee. Blinds you can pull down
to mute the sun. A screen charting where you're going
and all the places you've come from.

I wish my mind was this German train; efficient,
orderly, running on time. And all these thoughts
traveling to who knows where –
chattering-eating-sleeping, quietly crying
or lingering at the window, lost in the face staring back.

Traffic

And when they finally confirm
what you'd come to suspect
that you've spent your whole life
concealing her as best you could
starting with the unwritten rules
for little girls from rundown homes
who can't spell out sounds, who can't
sit still, or tell the time, or tie a lace
or hone the flit of their moth-headed ways
the persistent puzzle to fit the slot
its morphing shape, the falling short
the energy shift to stay composed
to bite her lip, to quash the impulse
to stim the glitch, to hold the dam
to stop the spew of speech unravelling
the heart of it, the bandwidth blip
the getting lost, a compass flipped,
a foreign map to read the codes
with light-too-bright sore eyes
the comfort zone that she can't take
beyond the door into the world
she doesn't suit, its buzz wire game
her bated breath, its constant bleeps
the bottleneck of incoming data
outgoing calls, the unruliness
of decibels, the traffic jam
inside her skull, the overwhelm-overdrive-overload
the *are you getting tired keeping up with this?*
I digress,
          where was I?
                              Yes –
when you finally understand
how you've spent your whole life
masking her like she's only *this*
and then you look, really look
at what she's given you and who she is –
let her stand up now. See her.
Here she is. Here.

Sharon on the Path

I was drawn to the shore today,
dropped my bags and headed out across the high, tumbling lawn,
its deep blue hydrangeas bordering a perfect line of sea.

And down the long winding path by the field, I found her,
my shepherd guide, a lone dog walker, who offered to show me
the way to where pebbles and sand kiss water.

And we walked and talked, and trusted, like the loosestrife
and blackberries flanking our way, that good things can bud
from nothing more than chance and nature, can pass

between two people when we amble down to the shore,
the pendulum to and fro, back and forth of lives shared
between a spitty, chewed-up ball.

And now here at this desk, I'm still holding
something of it all, will keep it held, remember us
still, and rooted to the sandy path, the wind

running its palm over the tall grass,
it's rippling bow to water,
the wet, bright joy of a dog.

Walk by the Thames

i.m Matilda (August – December 2007)

Tanja, so few moments we get these days to chew the fat.
You up from Brighton, me down from Sheff. Stopped here
on this bridge, we both know how it is now, memory's cargo
drifting, our histories floating somewhere out at sea.

But in this silence, we know too, some things
never diminish, never shrink, never become a speck
or sink from view. Whatever good it might do to know –
I still go back to answering that call at 3am,

to driving in the frost to search corridors and wards,
for that tiny cell-like room, where I find you cradling
your four-month-old girl. And everything is held
like breath inside the calm, impossible to grasp:

the nurse offering to dress her, then handing her back,
the police with their notepads checking on facts. Matilda.
Her face in repose, her tiny nose crowned by a bubble
of watery blood. Whatever good, in this shared stillness,

I'm still here, still there with you. Seeing a mother
emptying yourself of the milk that won't stop.
Bearing witness to everything that life isn't, and is.

On Upper Byron

you avoid the guy with knuckled eyes you met at The Sheaf
that time, stick your head in the boot whenever he walks past.
Over the road, they've painted their front door like a Tardis,
ready for when The Doctor visits Parkhill Flats. And up
in a bedroom window to the left sits the white Parlophone dog,

black ears pricked to the street, listening for his master's voice,
watching the bearded one who sits on his step staring out at No.3.
On Upper Byron, people leave out the things they don't want.
Today it's The Rough Guide to China, some red suede shoes,
an old soda stream. And Jill at 76 knows everyone's news.

That baking summer of chemo, when she knocked with slabs
of Victoria sponge. Always gardening with her grown-up son
who never speaks. So pleased when *Fag-ash Lil* moved out
from next door overnight, after her youngest went inside
the second time, a teardrop tattooed in the corner of his eye.

At No 42, Troy Boy the staffie has passed away and Barry's lost
a lot of weight. Over the back gate you compare treatment notes,
realise how long ago you made his daily trip, to *carpet bomb cells*
as Lynn called it. You picture Troy's stocky legs padding off
down the dark alley into the light. *End of an era* you say.

On Upper Byron, depending on the wind, you might hear
the roar of a goal at Bramall Lane, or be jolted awake
by a joyriding quadbike that cuts through your attic at night,
a police helicopter wasping the rooftops. And you might
find yourself looking down, seeing everything

from even higher, the street in railway miniature,
still and predictable, as if all of this never happened.

Before Diagnosis

After Anne Sexton

The rooms of my adult life were mostly filled
with too much furniture, no easy route
to countless unopened doors, external hard drives
stacked like tombstones on hardwood floors,
the odd rug not big enough to sprawl out on,
kindling in grates left unlit, folders of folders,
lists of lists, a library of blank notepads,
towers of unread books, dried up pens,
everything typed in CAPS, and more screens
than windows – their curtains routinely shut.
But mercifully, the one TV buried
underneath a desk. There were lots of desks,
one with a pillow for a keyboard, and a bed
with a keyboard for a pillow. And everywhere
the glare of blue-white light. I would go on,
but the detail's gone. I'd have to jog
my memory more by opening up cupboards
and doors for which the keys have disappeared
down the backs of lonely sofas
that were taken away in hospital green
removal vans. Some have been plastered up.
If I look carefully, I can see where they were
in the daylight that breathes through each room
like air into lungs. Now, there are new doors.
Doors I've yet to open, or walk through with a pen.
The one that takes me out into my garden –
that's my favourite.

Acknowledgements

Many thanks to the editors of the following publications and webzines where some of these poems, or versions of them, first appeared: *The Rialto, Under the Radar, Prole, Matter, Poetry Wales, Brittle Star, And Other Poems, Butcher's Dog, The North, Magma* and *Café Writers Magazine*. 'Ward 2' and 'Treatment' appeared in *Verse Matters* anthology (Valley Press 2017) edited by Rachel Bower & Helen Mort. 'Joy' and 'Sea Road' were republished in *The Untangling Anthology* (Arvon 2020). 'Soulmates (Inbox)' appeared in *Fragmented Voices* anthology (2020) edited by Natalie Crick, Natalie Nera & Rue Collinge.

'Lesley' won first place in the Prole Laureate Poetry Competition 2019. 'Walk by the Thames' was a runner up in the Mother's Milk Prize 2020. 'Treatment' was highly commended in the Carers UK Poetry Competition 2017. A version of this pamphlet was one of ten shortlisted in the *Magma* Pamphlet Competition 2020 judged by Mary Jean Chan.

A big thank you to Arvon for their invaluable support over the last few years via the brilliant Arvon/Jerwood Mentoring Scheme, and its staff, past and present, who've also been a special part of my journey: Becky Swain, Joe Bibby and Sophie Lloyd-Catchpole. Thank you to Hannah Lowe for her sage mentoring support and wider generosity. Props also to my fellow poetry mentees Arji Manuelpillai and Jeff Sugarman.

I'm extremely grateful to all those who've encouraged and championed me and my poetry over the last few years, particularly: Nik Perring, Jonathan Edwards, Brett Evans, and my cherished poetry sisters: Ness Lampert, Warda Yassin, and Danae Wellington, for raising me up in the ways only sisters can.

I'd also like to thank the many other poets who've supported me along the way including: Brian Lewis, Cian Ferriter, Rachel Bower, Peter Sansom, Ian McMillan, Stuart Paterson, Colette Bryce, Julia Copus, Clare Shaw and John McAuliffe. From Table Poetry, thanks for astute feedback and insights from Suzannah Evans, Julian Dobson, Helen Angell and John Stocks.

Thank you also to the Munster Literature Centre and Southword Editions for their support of this honour, and to judges Maya C. Popa and James Harpur for believing in my work.

Much gratitude to my friends, and to my family for all you've taught me on surviving and striving, particularly to my sister, Lorna Jo, who is the reason I made something of myself. And finally, thank you to my young writer family who led me back to words and continue to inspire me.

Notes

In the poems *Mechanisms* and *Traffic*, the term *stim* refers to a self-stimulating or soothing behaviour, usually involving repetitive movements, sensations or sounds. Most people stim in some way, but it's often more prominent in people on the autism spectrum, or with Attention Deficit or sensory processing disorder.

Joy uses text from *A War on Joy* The Spectator, 27th May 2017. The last line is a quote from Rim, a young woman living under the Isis regime, taken from *Women of Raqqa* published by dw.com 6th April 2016.

Printed in Great Britain
by Amazon

60252721R00021